From Your Friends at *The Mailbox*®

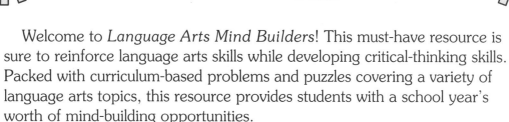

Language Arts
MIND BUILDERS

Grade 1

Welcome to *Language Arts Mind Builders*! This must-have resource is sure to reinforce language arts skills while developing critical-thinking skills. Packed with curriculum-based problems and puzzles covering a variety of language arts topics, this resource provides students with a school year's worth of mind-building opportunities.

Project Manager:
Njeri Jones Legrand

Editor:
Susan Walker

Writer:
Stacy Stone Davis

Art Coordinator:
Pam Crane

Artist:
Nolan Galloway

Cover Artists:
Nick Greenwood, Clevell Harris, Kimberly Richard

www.themailbox.com

©2001 by THE EDUCATION CENTER, INC.
All rights reserved.
ISBN #1-56234-419-6

Manufactured in the United States

10 9 8 7 6 5 4 3 2

INCLUDED IN THIS BOOK

Each activity page features five mind-building language arts problems plus a more difficult bonus builder problem to boost students' critical-thinking skills. Inside you will find an assortment of problems designed to reinforce the language arts skills that you teach. Featured topics and skills include the following:

- word skills
- writing

- reading
- proofreading

- grammar & usage

HOW TO USE THIS BOOK

Use the activity pages in this book in a variety of ways to supplement your language arts curriculum.

 For independent practice, duplicate the activity pages for students to use as morning work, problems of the day, free-time activities, or daily homework practice.

 For partner or small-group practice, duplicate the desired activity pages for each pair or group. Have students discuss possible answers for the problems.

 For whole-group practice, make transparencies of the activity pages.

 For a learning center activity, duplicate, laminate, and cut apart the activity pages. Group the resulting cards by topic and place specific skill cards at a center. Or, for a mixed review, place a variety of skill cards at a center.

 For assessing students' understanding of language arts concepts, make individual student copies and have each student explain in writing his thought process for answering each problem.

WORD SKILLS

Fill in the missing letters.

A a, B b, C c, D ___, E e, ___ f,

G ___, ___ h, I i

(1)

READING

Read the sentence.

The little dog ran away.

Write one reason why you think the dog ran away.

(2)

WRITING

Finish this sentence.

My teacher...

(3)

GRAMMAR & USAGE

List five nouns that begin with **b**.

(4)

PROOFREADING

Correct the sentence.

i like school.

(5)

BONUS BUILDER #1

Write two words that rhyme with *four.*

WORD SKILLS

WORD SKILLS

For each word below, write another word that begins with the same sound.

me   red   big
down   look

(6)

READING

Read the sentences.

Sam is a boy. He likes to play.

Who likes to play? Write your answer.

(7)

WRITING

List all the words that you think of when you see an apple.

(8)

GRAMMAR & USAGE

Which of the following does not belong? Explain why.

cat   dog   run   duck

(9)

PROOFREADING

Circle the misspelled word.

The house iz big.

(10)

BONUS BUILDER #2

Look at the nonsense words below.

gebe, hinky, fash, montop

Which one begins with the same sound as *goat*?

WORD SKILLS

©2001 The Education Center, Inc. • *Mind Builders* • *Language Arts* • TEC1603 • Key p. 45

WORD SKILLS

Write your name.
Circle all the consonants.

(11)

READING

Read.

Jon has a pole.
Jon has a worm.

What will Jon do next? Write your answer.

(12)

WRITING

Write a sentence about this picture.

(13)

GRAMMAR & USAGE

Circle the nouns. There are three.

The bird flew from the tree to the house.

(14)

PROOFREADING

Underline the word that should be capitalized.

tim is a boy.

(15)

BONUS BUILDER #3

Finish the poem.

I like to swing.
I like to play.
I like to _____
Every day.

WRITING

WORD SKILLS

Circle all the words that end with the same sound.

and   said   for

up   red

(16)

READING

Read the sentence.

Nan's hair is wet.

Write three reasons why Nan's hair might be wet.

(17)

WRITING

Finish these sentences.

I like to…

I don't like to…

(18)

GRAMMAR & USAGE

Put a box around each of the proper nouns. There are four.

Mary and Sam drove to Orlando, Florida.

(19)

PROOFREADING

Put the correct punctuation mark at the end of each sentence.

My dog is named Spot

What is your dog's name

(20)

BONUS BUILDER #4

Which of the following words does not belong? Explain why.

cat   fish   dog   bird   dish

WORD SKILLS

WORD SKILLS

Underline the words that rhyme.

bed
red
met
Ted
den

(21)

READING

Read the sentence.

Bill is glad.

Circle the sentences that could tell why Bill is glad.

He hurt his arm.
He got a pet cat.
He is going to the zoo.

(22)

WRITING

Write five words that tell about you.

(23)

GRAMMAR & USAGE

Circle the sentence that is correct.

Yesterday I seen a fish.
Yesterday I saw a fish.

(24)

PROOFREADING

Circle the mistakes. There are three.

i like to ete pizza?

(25)

BONUS BUILDER #5

Using the letters below, make as many words as possible.

Hint: Try to make at least ten words.

n, u, a, t, p

WORD SKILLS

WORD SKILLS

Write four words that rhyme with *at*.

26

READING

Read the sentences.

Jan got her lunch.
Jan got her bookbag.

Write a sentence telling where Jan might be going.

27

WRITING

Write two sentences that tell about your summer.

28

GRAMMAR & USAGE

Explain what a proper noun is.

29

PROOFREADING

Circle the sentence with no mistakes.

how old are you.
How old are you?

30

BONUS BUILDER #6

Read and solve the riddles.
I help you tell time.
I go ticktock.
I am a __ __ __ __ __.
I can be small or big.
I can float.
I am a __ __ __ __.

READING

WORD SKILLS

Church begins with *ch.*
Draw something else
that begins with *ch.*

(31)

READING

Read the sentence.

The pretty white cat ran after the dog.

Write why you think the cat ran after the dog.

(32)

WRITING

Pretend this bus can talk.
Write what the bus might say at the end of the day.

(33)

GRAMMAR & USAGE

Write an **n** next to each underlined noun.
Write a **v** next to each underlined verb.

1. The <u>boy</u> bought a gift.
2. My aunt <u>drives</u> a schoolbus.
3. The dog has brown <u>spots.</u>
4. I saw a bunny <u>eating</u> a carrot.

(34)

PROOFREADING

Correct this sentence. There are two mistakes.

jill can jump

(35)

BONUS BUILDER #7

Make a list of all the things you can do with a paper clip.

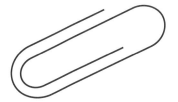

WRITING

WORD SKILLS

Write five words that have the sound of short **e.**

(36)

READING

Read the sentences.

Anna put on a wig.
Anna put on a mask.
Anna put on a funny dress.

What holiday do you think Anna is celebrating?

(37)

WRITING

Finish this sentence.

I like school because…

(38)

GRAMMAR & USAGE

Circle the proper nouns.

Lisa
Mike
doctor
city
Maine

(39)

PROOFREADING

Put the correct punctuation mark at the end of each sentence.

Jack will play with me
Will you play with me

(40)

BONUS BUILDER #8

Write a complete sentence. Use the words below.

funny	the
dog	bed
the	jumped
on	

WRITING

WORD SKILLS

Ship begins with *sh.*
Write five other words that begin with the sound *sh.*

41

READING

Read the sentences.

Pig put on his bathing suit.
Pig went to the lake.

Circle the sentence that tells what Pig might do next.

Pig will swim.
Pig will eat lunch.

42

WRITING

Write a sentence about your favorite food.

43

GRAMMAR & USAGE

Mary went to the store.
She rode her bike.

Who is <u>she</u>?

44

PROOFREADING

Circle the misspelled words. There are two.

Mi dad likes to du the dishes.

45

BONUS BUILDER #9

Circle all the short **a** words in this sentence.

Sam and Pat ran in a race last week.

WORD SKILLS

WORD SKILLS

For each word below, write a word that means the opposite.

come   wide
little   under
up

46

READING

Draw three trees.
Draw three red apples on the first tree.
Draw six oranges on the second tree.
Draw five purple plums on the third tree.

47

WRITING

Finish this sentence.

When I grow up, I want to be...

48

GRAMMAR & USAGE

Underline the verb in this sentence.

Sam rides a bike.

49

PROOFREADING

Correct the sentence. There are three mistakes.

i see a liffle Cut

50

BONUS BUILDER #10

Read the riddle.

I can be seen in the sky at night.
I'm sometimes big, round, and bright.

What am I?

READING

©2001 The Education Center, Inc. • *Mind Builders* • Language Arts • TEC1603 • Key p. 45

WORD SKILLS

Write these words in ABC order.

too
see
now
all
for

(51)

READING

Read the story.

Mop is my cat. Mop likes to play with me. Mop sleeps at the end of my bed.

Circle the best title for this story.

Mop the Floor
My Cat, Mop
Cats Are Fun

(52)

WRITING

Write two sentences about this creature.

(53)

GRAMMAR & USAGE

Write three proper nouns that could complete this sentence.

My dad drove to_____.

(54)

PROOFREADING

Circle all the words that should be capitalized.

nan   mr.
boy   dog
town

(55)

BONUS BUILDER #11

Write four sentences that tell about your family.

WRITING

WORD SKILLS

Underline the words that have the sound of short **i.**

in
ride
this
did
find

56

READING

Write these sentences in order.

Mom frosted the cake.
Mom mixed the cake.
Mom baked the cake.

57

WRITING

If you could take a trip on a flying carpet, where would you go? Write a story.

58

GRAMMAR & USAGE

Put a check mark by the correct sentence. Put an X by the incorrect sentence.

My dog hurted his paw.
My dog hurt his paw.

59

PROOFREADING

Correct the sentence. There are three mistakes.

my dog spot hid under the big bed

60

BONUS BUILDER #12

Fill in the chart with synonyms for *big*.

big

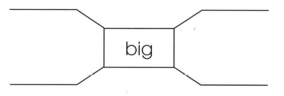

WORD SKILLS

WORD SKILLS

Here is a riddle.

  I am big.
  I move in the water.
  My beginning sound is the same
    as in *sheep*.

  What am I?
  I am a __ __ __ __.

61

READING

Read the sentences.

  Jake puts on a hat.
  He puts on a suit.
  He hops on a truck.
  He uses a hose.

What is Jake's job?

62

WRITING

Look at this picture.

Write a sentence
telling where
you think the
girl is going.

63

GRAMMAR & USAGE

Write five nouns that would make
sense in this sentence.

  The little boy went to the

  _____.

64

PROOFREADING

Circle the sentence that has no
mistakes.

  I like to read books.
  mi best color is red

65

BONUS BUILDER #13

Read the sentences.
Write **1, 2,** and **3** to put these
sentences in order.

  Joe got into bed.
  Joe went to sleep.
  Joe put on his pajamas.

READING

WORD SKILLS

Change the first letter in each of the words below to make another short **o** word.

hop
pot
cob
hog

66

READING

Read.

The girl got a plate.
The girl put food on the plate.
She sat down.

Draw a picture to show what the girl probably did next.

67

WRITING

List different toppings that can be put on pizza.
Put a star by your favorite topping.

68

GRAMMAR & USAGE

Make each of the words below plural.

toy   egg
dog   bike
cat

69

PROOFREADING

Correct this sentence. There are four mistakes.

where Are you Going

70

BONUS BUILDER #14

Put these words into two groups. Give each group a title. Explain how you grouped the words.

red   white   three
green   two   eight
black   ten   one
brown

READING

WORD SKILLS

Circle the words that are not spelled correctly.

and   uv
mi   the
to

(71)

READING

Read the sentence.

Susan was late for school yesterday.

Write five reasons why Susan could have been late.

(72)

WRITING

Write a story telling what you think is in this box.

(73)

GRAMMAR & USAGE

List five verbs that tell you what you might do in a day.

(74)

PROOFREADING

Underline the words that should begin with a capital letter. There are three words.

sue lives in smithville, virginia.

(75)

BONUS BUILDER #15

Look at the underlined words. Which underlined word means the same as *little*?
Circle that sentence.

The <u>tiny</u> mouse ran into the hole.
The <u>scared</u> mouse ran away.

WORD SKILLS

WORD SKILLS

Rearrange each set of letters to make a short **u** word.

urb
pu
nuf
bgu
usn

76

READING

Read the directions to make a pumpkin.

Draw a circle on your paper.
Draw a rectangle stem.
Draw two triangle eyes.
Draw a square nose.
Draw a happy smile.

77

WRITING

Finish this poem.

Red apples, red leaves,
Red mittens, red trees.
Red is everywhere!
Red candy, red sky,
Red _____, red
_____.
Red is everywhere!

78

GRAMMAR & USAGE

Circle the word in this sentence that needs to be corrected.

I am the tall person in my class.

79

PROOFREADING

Put the correct punctuation at the end of each sentence.

My horse likes to run
I have two sisters
Do you like corn

80

BONUS BUILDER #16

For each word below, write a word that means the opposite.

after   open
give   stop
old

WORD SKILLS

©2001 The Education Center, Inc. • *Mind Builders* • Language Arts • TEC1603 • Key p. 46

WORD SKILLS

Circle all the words that rhyme with "said."

red	bed	maid
head	paid	fed

(81)

READING

Read the sentences.
Circle the event that happened first.

Nick felt cold.
Nick went outside without a coat.

(82)

WRITING

Write a story about your favorite holiday.

(83)

GRAMMAR & USAGE

List five verbs that would make sense in this sentence.

The little girl _____ on the train.

(84)

PROOFREADING

Correct the sentence. There are two mistakes.

adam's birthday is in november.

(85)

BONUS BUILDER #17

Decide if the **y** in each word says **ē** or **ī**.
Write **e** or **i** next to each word.

any	try
every	silly
bunny	why

WORD SKILLS

WORD SKILLS

Read the words below.
Look at each underlined vowel.
Change the vowel to make a new word.

h<u>o</u>p   b<u>e</u>g
t<u>i</u>n   p<u>e</u>n
tr<u>u</u>ck

(86)

READING

Read the sentences.
Write **1, 2,** or **3** by each sentence to put them in order.

Lu got on her bike.
Lu rode her bike down the street.
Lu walked to her bike.

(87)

WRITING

Soup is good to eat on a cold day.
Write a recipe for a new kind of soup.

(88)

GRAMMAR & USAGE

Which of the following words does not belong?
Explain why.

hop   skip   boy   run   jump

(89)

PROOFREADING

Circle the misspelled words in this sentence. There are two.

Ware are yu going with that box?

(90)

BONUS BUILDER #18

Look at each underlined word.
Decide if it is a noun or a verb.
Write n or v in the box.

☐ The bird can <u>fly</u>.
☐ The <u>fly</u> landed on the table.
☐ That dog can really <u>bark</u>!
☐ The <u>bark</u> is peeling off the tree.

GRAMMAR & USAGE

WORD SKILLS

Circle the words that have the sound of long **a**.

had   as
ate   make
take

91

READING

Read the story.

Tip is a dog. Tip likes to run.
Tip likes to play. Tip is a good dog!

Underline the best title for this story.

Playing Is Fun
Tip, the Dog
One Sunny Day

92

WRITING

Write what you think this bear is saying to the girl.

93

GRAMMAR & USAGE

Read the sentences.

I like baseball. It is a fun game.

What game is fun? Write your answer.

94

PROOFREADING

Draw an **X** over the letters that should not be capitalized.

Nancy And Carol Went To Seattle, Washington.

95

BONUS BUILDER #19

Pretend you are writing an ad for a new teacher. Make a list of qualities a teacher should have.

WRITING

WORD SKILLS

Put a box around the words spelled with a **c** that sounds like **k**.

once   could
can   city
come

96

READING

Read the sentence.

Sandra has very cold hands.

Write five reasons why Sandra's hands might be cold.

97

WRITING

Pretend you made a snowman that can talk. Write a story telling what it might say.

98

GRAMMAR & USAGE

Circle the following sentences that are statements.

My dog likes to run.
Can you run fast?
My sister is a fast runner.

99

PROOFREADING

Circle the correct sentence.

In july, matt took a trip to florida.
In July, matt took a trip to Florida.
In July, Matt took a trip to Florida.

100

In each row of letters, circle the hidden short-vowel word.

c d p a n g h u
j i h i t m n a
v n m b e t p l
t u b p o l j w

WORD SKILLS

WORD SKILLS

Finish each sentence with a word that has the sound of long **e**.

When you look around, what do you
___ ___ ___?

I was two, but now I am
___ ___ ___ ___ ___.

I picked an apple from the
___ ___ ___.

(101)

READING

Read the sentences.

Buddy went outside.
He looked in the mailbox.
There were two letters!

What do you think Buddy will do next?

(102)

WRITING

Write three things that you should do to care for your teeth.

(103)

GRAMMAR & USAGE

List five verbs that begin with the letter **h**.

(104)

PROOFREADING

Read the sentence.
Underline the words that need to be capitalized. There are four.

christmas, hanukkah, and kwanzaa are celebrated in december.

(105)

BONUS BUILDER #21

Pretend you are the teacher.
Put a star next to each word that is spelled correctly.

1. can   5. like   8. by
2. came   6. must   9. hiz
3. do   7. kno   10. aney
4. eet

WORD SKILLS

WORD SKILLS

Circle the words in which the **y** makes the sound of **ī**.

away	pretty
funny	by
my	fly

(106)

READING

Read the sentences.

Paul and Mia saw an elephant.
They ate peanuts and popcorn.
They saw clowns.

Where are Paul and Mia?

(107)

WRITING

Make a list of the things you do before school each day.

(108)

GRAMMAR & USAGE

Circle the correct sentence.

I am big than Jim.
I am bigger than Jim.

(109)

PROOFREADING

Correct the sentence. There are four mistakes.

for breakfast i had eggs bacon toast, and juice.

(110)

BONUS BUILDER #22

Make a list of different ways eggs can be cooked.

WRITING

WORD SKILLS

Rearrange each set of letters to make a long **o** word.

og
nobe
kwno
ocen
oet

(111)

READING

Read the schedule. Then answer the question.

Which event takes place at noon?

Town Celebration
Parade—9:00
Clowns in the Park—10:30
Carnival—12:00
Games—1:30
Picnic—3:00
Music—6:00
Fireworks—9:30

(112)

WRITING

Write a story about what you might find at the end of a rainbow.

(113)

GRAMMAR & USAGE

Read the sentences.

Dan is a boy.
<u>Dan</u> likes to run and play.

In the second sentence, what word could take the place of *Dan?* Write that word.

(114)

PROOFREADING

Explain why this sentence is not correct.

my brother jim likes to dance and play the drums

(115)

BONUS BUILDER #23

Bat is a word that has more than one meaning.

A <u>bat</u> is an animal.
A <u>bat</u> is used to hit a baseball.

List at least three other words that have more than one meaning.

WORD SKILLS

WORD SKILLS

Look at the words below. Match a word from each column to make a compound word.

butter	bow
play	fly
foot	shine
sun	ground
rain	ball

116

READING

Read the sentences.

My <u>beebat</u> is soft and furry.
My <u>beebat</u> likes to drink milk.
My <u>beebat</u> likes to play with yarn.
My <u>beebat</u> purrs loudly when I pet her.

What is a <u>beebat</u>? Circle one.

dog   horse   fish   cat

117

WRITING

Write three questions you would like to ask a tree.

118

GRAMMAR & USAGE

Circle the words that could be both a noun and a verb.

fly
bark
sun
fish
dirt

119

PROOFREADING

Draw a star next to the sentence that has no mistakes.

Fran likes to sing.
fran like to sing

120

BONUS BUILDER #24

Your friend asked you to read this note. He wants you to check it for mistakes. Circle the mistakes that you find.

Mom,
i went to the store with grandma. we will get eggs. milk. and bread. We will be back by 2:00? sec you then.

WORD SKILLS

Put a box around each of the words that have the sound of long **u.**

put
tube
buy
jump
mule

(121)

READING

Read the sentence.

Maria just finished reading a book.

Write five things that could happen next.

(122)

WRITING

Here is an invention. Write about it.

(123)

GRAMMAR & USAGE

Here is a picture of a mouse. List as many adjectives as possible that can describe the mouse.

(124)

PROOFREADING

Correct the sentence. There are three mistakes.

my sisters friend lost a tooth

(125)

BONUS BUILDER #25

Circle the names that are written correctly.

dr. Benjamin D. Levine
Miss Emily Taggart
mrs. sheehan
Mr. john Bragg
Dr. Timersol

PROOFREADING

WORD SKILLS

Write the names of five storybook characters.
Put their names in ABC order.

(126)

READING

Read the sentence.

The colors of the rainbow are red, orange, yellow, green, blue, indigo, and violet.

Write the number word that tells how many colors there are in the rainbow.

(127)

WRITING

Pretend your favorite storybook character is coming for lunch. Write a menu telling what you would serve.

(128)

GRAMMAR & USAGE

Read the sentence.

The pretty brown horse trotted through the meadow

Circle the two nouns.
Underline the verb.
Put boxes around the adjectives.

(129)

PROOFREADING

Circle each sentence that has the correct punctuation mark.

Ouch, my toe hurts?
Did you remember to feed the dog?
Can you fly a kite?

(130)

BONUS BUILDER #26

If you had three wishes, what would you wish for? Write your three wishes.

WRITING

WORD SKILLS

For each word below, underline the consonant blend.
Write another word that has the same beginning blend.

trap   smile
stop   flip
from

(131)

READING

Read the clues.

I can not run.
I can swim.
I live in the sea.
I am very, very big.
I am a mammal.

What am I?
Draw a picture of me.

(132)

WRITING

List at least five
different places
where you might
see a computer.

(133)

GRAMMAR & USAGE

Read the sentence below.

The giant is <u>gentle</u>.

Take out the word *gentle*.
List five different adjectives to
describe the giant.

(134)

PROOFREADING

Correct the sentence. There are
four mistakes.

on friday it was snowing so hard
that i couldnt see out the
window.

(135)

BONUS BUILDER #27

Finish each sentence.
Write a word that rhymes with the
underlined word.

I ate and <u>ate</u> off my _ _ _ _ _.
I fell on the <u>floor</u>, then ran out the _ _ _ _!
I cracked an <u>egg</u> on my _ _ _.
You're so <u>bright</u>, that I know you're
_ _ _ _ _!

WORD SKILLS

WORD SKILLS

List at least five words that rhyme with *boat.*

(136)

READING

Which sentences might be in a story called "A Day at the Beach"? Put an **X** by each one.

Nick and Kari ran in the waves.
They made a sand castle.
The horse ran into the barn.
We ate a picnic lunch on the sand.

(137)

WRITING

Write a story about what hatches from this egg.

(138)

GRAMMAR & USAGE

Circle the sentence in which the word *fish* is used as a verb.

Wow, that <u>fish</u> is huge!
I like to <u>fish</u> in the pond.

(139)

PROOFREADING

Underline the words that need to be capitalized.

dr.
america
flag
washington
chicago

(140)

BONUS BUILDER #28

Read the riddle.

What's black and white and has 16 wheels?

Make up an answer to this riddle.

WRITING

WORD SKILLS

Write each word with the *-ing* ending added to it.

go   run
play   come
make   jump

(141)

READING

Read the story. What word is missing? Write it.

I like _____. _____ are funny.

_____ like to roll in the mud.

_____ oink and squeal.

(142)

WRITING

Write a short letter to your school librarian. Tell the librarian which library book is your favorite and why.

(143)

GRAMMAR & USAGE

Circle the words that have the same meaning.

little   tiny
small   funny
pretty   huge

(144)

PROOFREADING

Write the correct punctuation mark at the end of each sentence.

Wow, look at that pretty flower

Did you lose a tooth yesterday

(145)

BONUS BUILDER #29

Read each sentence below. Unscramble the letters to fill in the blank.

1. I am big and red. Animals sleep in me. I am a _____. brna
2. I am yellow. I taste good. I grow on a cob. I am _____. cnor

READING

WORD SKILLS

Put a star by each word that is spelled correctly.
Then correctly spell the misspelled words.

like	sed
hav	you
look	do

(146)

READING

Match each phrase in column **A** to a phrase in column **B** to make a complete sentence.

A	**B**
The little bird	walked to the store.
The man	swam in the water.
The pretty fish	flew to its nest.

(147)

WRITING

Write a story about an imaginary trip to outer space.

(148)

GRAMMAR & USAGE

Write each of the following words in plural form.

boy
fox
eye
wish
church

(149)

PROOFREADING

Underline the mistakes in this address. There are six mistakes.

jane smith
414 main street
jonesburg, virginia 41433

(150)

BONUS BUILDER #30

In each row, circle the hidden long-vowel word.

r e p l a t e d
l m k i t e m n
r f i d f e e t
m n h o p e w s
m u l e p o d c

WORD SKILLS

WORD SKILLS

Circle the words that have a long-vowel sound.

Underline the words that have a short-vowel sound.

well	be
under	stop
say	just

(151)

READING

Draw five eggs.
Color one egg blue.
Give one egg green stripes.
Give one egg red dots.
Color one egg yellow.
Color one egg orange.

(152)

WRITING

Make a list of all the things you should take with you when you go on a picnic.

(153)

GRAMMAR & USAGE

Name one family member. Write five adjectives to describe that person.

(154)

PROOFREADING

Put a star by the sentence that is written correctly.

Yesterday I ate a ham, burger, french, fries, and a milk, shake.
Yesterday I ate a hamburger, french fries, and a milkshake.

(155)

BONUS BUILDER #31

Underline the following sentences that state an opinion.

Chocolate is the best flavor for ice cream.
Robins can fly.
Mr. Smith is the kindest teacher in the school.
January is the nicest month of the year.

READING

WORD SKILLS

For each word below, circle the consonant blend.
Write another word that has the same beginning blend.

swing
blue
prince

gray
skin

(156)

READING

Read the sentences.

Once there was a horse. The horse liked to run. The horse liked to gallop in the field. The horse liked to rest in its stall.

Circle the best title for this story.

The Busy Horse
The Red Barn
A Pretty Meadow

(157)

WRITING

Write five facts about your favorite animal.

(158)

GRAMMAR & USAGE

Circle the words that are plural.

dishes
gas
girls
car
tires

(159)

PROOFREADING

Put quotation marks where they are needed.

Tom asked, Would you like to go to the zoo with me?

(160)

BONUS BUILDER #32

Circle **a** or **an** to complete each sentence.

I would like to have (a, an) dog.
Will you eat (a, an) banana?
I have (a, an) earache.
I saw (a, an) elephant at the zoo.

GRAMMAR & USAGE

WORD SKILLS

For each word below, change the underlined vowel to make a new word.

m<u>i</u>le   m<u>i</u>ne

t<u>a</u>me   l<u>a</u>ke

c<u>o</u>ne

(161)

READING

Read the story; then answer the questions.

Spiders
Did you know that spiders are not insects? Spiders are arachnids. Spiders have eight legs. Some spiders have four, six, or even eight eyes! Spiders are very interesting.

How many eyes do spiders have? Are spiders insects?

(162)

WRITING

Write about the funniest thing that has ever happened to you.

(163)

GRAMMAR & USAGE

Read the sentences. Put a star by the sentence that is written in the past tense.

My brother broke his leg.
My sister is swimming in the lake.

(164)

PROOFREADING

Put commas in this sentence. Four commas are needed.

Joe Tim Ron, and Nan went to the store to buy balloons plates cups, and spoons.

(165)

BONUS BUILDER #33

Here is a picture of a new kind of sneaker. Write at least five sentences about it.
Be sure to tell what special things it can do.

WRITING

WORD SKILLS

Circle the contractions in each sentence.
Write the two words that make up each contraction.

Nan didn't eat her apple.
Fran can't see the bus.
It's Dan's birthday today.

166

READING

Read the sentences.

On April Fools' Day, Mary told Sue that here was a real giraffe in school. Sue said to Mary, "I think you're pulling my leg! There's no giraffe in school."

Explain what it means if you are pulling someone's leg.

167

WRITING

Make a list of different uses for an empty coffee can.

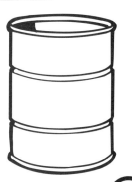

168

GRAMMAR & USAGE

Circle the sentence that contains a possessive.

Sue's dresses are all red.
That's my ball.

169

PROOFREADING

Circle the misspelled words in this sentence. There are four.

Wonce I saw a liddle bird fli away frum a cat.

170

BONUS BUILDER #34

Circle the words that could describe the cat in this sentence.

My _____ cat runs fast.

furry   quickly
happy   loud
black

GRAMMAR & USAGE

   ©2001 The Education Center, Inc. • *Mind Builders • Language Arts* • TEC1603 • Key p. 47

WORD SKILLS

For each word below, circle the letter that is silent.

ride
boat
make
play
paid

(171)

READING

Read and solve the riddle.

You can drink this.
This can be warm when you drink it.
This can be cold when you drink it.
You can float in it.
A ship can sail in it.
You can clean things with it.

What is it?

(172)

WRITING

Write a thank-you note to one of your classmates. Thank your classmate for doing something nice for you.

(173)

GRAMMAR & USAGE

Underline the sentence in which the word *play* is used as a noun.

Will you <u>play</u> with me?
I want to go see the <u>play</u>.

(174)

PROOFREADING

Correct this sentence. There are six mistakes.

would you like to take a trip to hawaii california, or florida

(175)

BONUS BUILDER #35

Read each sentence. Circle the sentence if the underlined word is used correctly.

The <u>night</u> helped the queen.
The moon can be seen at <u>night</u>.
I don't <u>know</u> the answer.
I have <u>know</u> more paper.

WORD SKILLS

WORD SKILLS

Read the sentence below. Circle the words that sound alike but are spelled differently.

I came here to hear the band play.

(176)

READING

Read the sentences. Fill in the blanks to make a story.

Once there was a little frog. The _____ did not like to jump. The frog did not _____ to hop. Day after _____ the little frog just sat on a lily pad. The _____ frog did nothing but catch flies!

(177)

WRITING

Write a conversation between these two children. Be sure to use quotation marks.

(178)

GRAMMAR & USAGE

Circle the sentence that has the most adjectives.

Jill ate four red apples.
Josh walked three blocks.

(179)

PROOFREADING

Put the correct punctuation mark at the end of each sentence.

How old wIll you be on your next birthday
What time is it
My father likes to bake bread

(180)

BONUS BUILDER #36

Read each sentence. Draw a circle around the sentences that state a fact.

There are 12 months in a year.
Pizza House makes the best pizza!
Snickers® is the best candy bar.
George Washington was the first president.

READING

WORD SKILLS

Look at the words below. Match words from each column that have the same meaning.

big	tiny
funny	ill
small	huge
scared	silly
sick	frightened

(181)

READING

Read the recipe.

Lemonade
1 cup lemon juice
1 cup sugar
6 cups cold water
Pour the lemon juice into a pitcher.
Add the sugar. Pour in the water. Stir.

What do you do after you add the sugar?

(182)

WRITING

Write a story at least six sentences long to go with this title.

The Backward Day

(183)

GRAMMAR & USAGE

List at least three words that could complete this sentence.

The firemen _____ drove to the scene of the fire.

(184)

PROOFREADING

Correct this sentence. There are five mistakes.

i ordered a sundae with syrup whipped cream nuts sprinkles, and a cherry on top

(185)

BONUS BUILDER #37

Write one of the following words in each of these sentences.

to   two   too

My brother is _____years old.
I am going _____ a party.
She will go to the party, _____!

WORD SKILLS

WORD SKILLS

What two words make up each contraction? Write them.

it's
can't
she'll
we'll
won't

(186)

READING

Read the short story.

Once upon a time, there was a princess. She lived in a castle with lots of gold and toys. But the princess was lonely. One day she met a frog. The frog asked the princess to play. The princess had a new friend.

Name the main character of this story.

(187)

WRITING

Write a letter to your future teacher. Tell the teacher things you like about school.

(188)

GRAMMAR & USAGE

Circle the sentences with verbs in the present tense.

Chip plays in the woods.
Kari fell out of bed last night.
He reads books.

(189)

PROOFREADING

Explain what is wrong with this sentence.

Mrs. Smith said, please don't pick the flowers.

(190)

Write a note to your teacher. Tell why you like being a student in his or her class.

WORD SKILLS

Count the syllables in each word. Write the number of syllables next to each word.

summer   wagon
rain   envelope
apple

191

READING

Where might you see a sign like this?

Schedule
Bus 1 departs 2:00 P.M.
Bus 2 departs 3:30 P.M.
Bus 3 departs 5:00 P.M.
Bus 4 departs 6:30 P.M.

192

WRITING

Write instructions for making your favorite sandwich.

193

GRAMMAR & USAGE

Circle the correct pronoun that should be used in each sentence.

Victor put _____ cake in the oven.
           his I

Mrs. Conor took _____ sister to a party.
           she her

194

PROOFREADING

Write the sentence correctly. There are three mistakes.

my grandmother made cookies cake, and lemonade?

195

BONUS BUILDER #39

Circle the words spelled with a **c** that sounds like an **s.**

cent
celery
carrot
cable
pace

WORD SKILLS

WORD SKILLS

Circle the words that have matching long-vowel sounds.

weed   tree
seat   toe
pail   tube

(196)

READING

Read the sentences.

Jenna put on some sunscreen.
She filled a pail with sand.
Then she jumped and
    played in the waves.

Where is Jenna?

(197)

WRITING

Finish this sentence.

The six fat sheep said, "…

(198)

GRAMMAR & USAGE

Cross out the word that is not needed in each sentence.

Tomas he cleaned his fish tank.
Alex doesn't not have his own
    room.

(199)

PROOFREADING

Circle the word that is spelled correctly.

anser
answer
ansor

(200)

BONUS BUILDER #40

Circle the word in each pair that is spelled correctly.

botc   boat
snail   snale
tube   toob
trea   tree

WORD SKILLS

WORD SKILLS

Write each word pair as a contraction.

is not   he will
they are   have not
it is   will not

201

READING

Is the following story reality or fantasy?

Sam is the best dancing fish in the pond. When he dances, all the pond animals clap and cheer. They all wish they could dance like Sam.

202

WRITING

Write questions you would ask your dad or mom about his or her job.

203

GRAMMAR & USAGE

Circle the nouns that are plural.

bus
mice
boxes
clock
cars

204

PROOFREADING

Circle the incorrect word in each sentence.

Jamal talking on the phone for an hour.
Tony put on his helmet and ride his bike.
Amy is swims faster than Carl.

205

BONUS BUILDER #41

Which word does not belong? Explain why.

big
pretty
horse
short
green

WORD SKILLS

WORD SKILLS

Underline the words that have a long-vowel sound. Circle the words that have a short-vowel sound.

bread   steam
meat   dream
head

(206)

READING

Read the sentence.

   Cassy knew the song by heart.

What do the words "by heart" mean?

(207)

WRITING

Write a paragraph to describe this picture.

(208)

GRAMMAR & USAGE

Put a box around the adverb in each sentence.

   Jordan quickly stood up.
   Max walked slowly to the front of the room.
   Andrew smoothly spread the frosting on the cake.

(209)

PROOFREADING

Circle the sentence that is correct.

   The brown dog ran quickly to the park.
   my best friend jan ran quickly around the playground

(210)

BONUS BUILDER #42

Circle the words that have the same vowel sound as *cow*.

soup
couch
cloud
cold

WORD SKILLS

Answer Keys

Page 3
1. A a, B b, C c, D **d**, E e, **F** f, G **g**, **H** h, I i
2. Answers may vary.
3. Answers may vary.
4. Answers may vary. (Examples: bat, bun, bear, bell, bone)
5. I like school.
Bonus Builder #1: Answers may vary. (Examples: door, roar, store, floor)

Page 4
6. Answers may vary.
7. Sam likes to play.
8. Answers may vary. (Examples: red, green, yellow, crunch, juicy, eat, fruit, tree)
9. run; It is a verb. The other words are nouns or animals.
10. The house (iz) big.
Bonus Builder #2: gebe

Page 5
11. Answers may vary.
12. Jon may go fishing.
13. Answers may vary.
14. The (bird) flew from the (tree) to the (house).
15. <u>Tim</u> is a boy.
Bonus Builder #3: Answers may vary.

Page 6
16. and, up, (said), (red), for
17. Answers may vary.
18. Answers may vary.
19. [Mary] and [Sam] drove to [Orlando], [Florida].
20. My dog is named Spot.
    What is your dog's name?
Bonus Builder #4: Dish does not belong. It is not an animal.

Page 7
21. <u>bed</u>, <u>red</u>, met, <u>Ted</u>, den
22. He hurt his arm.
    (He got a pet cat.)
    (He is going to the zoo.)
23. Answers may vary.
24. Yesterday I seen a fish.
    (Yesterday I saw a fish.)
25. (i) like to (ete) pizza(?)
Bonus Builder #5: Answers may vary. (Possible answers: an, at, up, nap, nut, pan, pat, put, tan, tap, pant, punt, tuna)

Page 8
26. Answers may vary. (Examples: cat, hat, mat, rat, sat, flat)
27. Answers may vary. (Possible answer: Jan is going to school.)
28. Answers may vary.
29. A proper noun names a specific person, place, or thing like Sue, Chicago, and July.
30. how old are you.
    (How old are you?)
Bonus Builder #6: clock, boat

Page 9
31. Answers may vary. (Possible drawings: chair, chain, chimney, chicken, chalk, chipmunk, chimpanzee, child)
32. Answers may vary.
33. Answers may vary.
34. 1. The <u>boy</u> bought a gift. n   3. The dog has brown <u>spots</u>. n
    2. My aunt <u>drives</u> a schoolbus. v   4. I saw a bunny <u>eating</u> a carrot. v
35. Jill can jump.
Bonus Builder #7: Answers may vary.

Page 10
36. Answers may vary. (Possible answers: hen, pen, ten, let, pet, wet)
37. Halloween
38. Answers may vary.
39. (Lisa), (Mike), doctor, city, (Maine)
40. Jack will play with me.
    Will you play with me?
Bonus Builder #8: Answers may vary. (Example: The funny dog jumped on the bed.)

Page 11
41. Answers may vary. (Examples: shark, shoe, show, sheet, shirt, shop)
42. (Pig will swim.)
    Pig will eat lunch.
43. Answers may vary.
44. Mary
45. (Mi) dad likes to (du) the dishes.
Bonus Builder #9: (Sam) (and) (Pat) (ran) in a race (last) week.

Page 12
46. Answers may vary. Possible answers are listed.
    come—go
    little—big
    up—down
    wide—narrow
    under—over
47. Drawings should match description.
48. Answers may vary.
49. Sam <u>rides</u> a bike.
50. I see a little cat.
Bonus Builder #10: the moon

Page 13
51. all, for, now, see, too
52. Mop the Floor
    (My Cat, Mop)
    Cats Are Fun
53. Answers may vary.
54. Answers may vary. (Examples: Chicago, Texas, Elk's Zoo)
55. (nan), boy, town, (mr.), dog
Bonus Builder #11: Answers may vary.

Page 14
56. <u>in</u>, ride, <u>this</u>, <u>did</u>, find
57. Mom mixed the cake.
    Mom baked the cake.
    Mom frosted the cake.
58. Answers may vary.
59. My dog hurted his paw. X
    My dog hurt his paw. ✓
60. My dog Spot hid under the big bed.
Bonus Builder #12: Answers may vary.

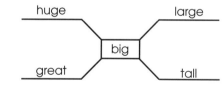

Page 15
61. ship
62. Jake is a firefighter.
63. Answers may vary.
64. Answers may vary. (Examples: zoo, store, playground, party, parade)
65. (I like to read books.)
    mi best color is red
Bonus Builder #13:
    2—Joe got into bed.
    3—Joe went to sleep.
    1—Joe put on his pajamas.

Answer Keys

Page 16

66. Answers may vary. Examples:
    hop—pop, top   cob—rob, sob
    pot—cot, hot   hog—dog, log
67. Answers may vary.
68. Answers may vary.
69. toys, dogs, cats, eggs, bikes
70. Where are you going?

Bonus Builder #14:
    numbers: one, two, three, eight, ten
    colors: white, green, black, red, brown
    They are grouped by numbers and colors.

Page 17

71. and, (mi), to, (uv), the
72. Answers may vary.
73. Answers may vary.
74. Answers may vary. (Examples: run, eat, work, play, read)
75. sue lives in smithville, virginia.

Bonus Builder #15: (The tiny mouse ran into the hole.)
        The scared mouse ran away.

Page 18

76. rub, up, fun, bug, sun
77. Drawings should match description.
78. Answers may vary.
79. I am the (tall) person in my class.
80. My horse likes to run.
    I have two sisters.
    Do you like corn?

Bonus Builder #16: Answers may vary. Possible answers:
    after—before   open—close
    give—take   stop—go
    old—new

Page 19

81. (red), (bed), maid, (head), paid, (fed)
82. Nick felt cold.
    (Nick went outside without a coat.)
83. Answers may vary.
84. Answers may vary. (Examples: rode, sang, ran, talked, stood)
85. Adam's birthday is in November.

Bonus Builder #17:
    any—e   try—i
    every—e   silly—e
    bunny—e   why—i

Page 20

86. Answers may vary. Examples:
    hop—hip
    tin—tan, ton, ten
    truck—track, trick
    beg—bag, big, bog, bug
    pen—pan, pin, pun
87. 2—Lu got on her bike.
    3—Lu rode her bike down the street.
    1—Lu walked to her bike.
88. Answers may vary.
89. boy; It is not a verb.
90. (Ware) are (yu) going with that box?

Bonus Builder #18:
    v—The bird can fly.   v—That dog can really bark!
    n—The fly landed on the table.   n—The bark is peeling off the tree.

Page 21

91. had, (ate), (take), as, (make)
92. Playing Is Fun
    Tip, The Dog
    One Sunny Day
93. Answers may vary.
94. baseball
95. Nancy ✗And Carol ✗Went ✗To Seattle, Washington.

Bonus Builder #19: Answers may vary.

Page 22

96. once, can, come, could, city
97. Answers may vary.
98. Answers may vary.
99. (My dog likes to run.)
    Can you run fast?
    (My sister is a fast runner.)
100. In july, matt took a trip to florida.
    In July, matt took a trip to Florida.
    (In July, Matt took a trip to Florida.)

Bonus Builder #20:
    c d (p a n) g h u
    j i (h i t) m n a
    v n m (b e t) p l
    (t u b) p o l j w

Page 23

101. When you look around, what do you __s__ __e__ __e__?
    I was two, but now I am __t__ __h__ __r__ __e__ __e__.
    I picked an apple from the __t__ __r__ __e__ __e__.
102. Answers may vary.
103. Answers may vary.
104. Answers may vary. (Examples: hop, hum, hold, hit, hear)
105. christmas, hanukkah, and kwanzaa are celebrated in december.

Bonus Builder #21:
    1. ★ can   6. ★ must
    2. ★ came   7. kno
    3. ★ do   8. ★ by
    4. eet   9. hiz
    5. ★ like   10. aney

Page 24

106. away, funny, (my), pretty, (by), (fly)
107. at the circus
108. Answers may vary.
109. I am big than Jim.
    (I am bigger than Jim.)
110. For breakfast I had eggs, bacon, toast, and juice.

Bonus Builder #22: Answers may vary.

Page 25

111. go, bone, know, cone, toe
112. the carnival
113. Answers may vary.
114. He
115. The first word in the sentence should be capitalized. The name Jim should be capitalized. The sentence should end with a period.

Bonus Builder #23: Answers may vary. (Examples: play, fly, slip)

Page 26

116. butter   bow
     play   fly
     foot   shine
     sun   ground
     rain   ball
117. dog   horse   fish   (cat)
118. Answers may vary.
119. (fly), (bark), (sun), (fish), dirt
120. ★ Fran likes to sing.
    fran like to sing

Bonus Builder #24:
Mom,
    (i) went to the store with (g)randma. (w)e will get eggs○ milk○ and bread. We will be back by 2:00(?) (s)ee you then.

Page 27

121. put, tube, buy, jump, mule
122. Answers may vary.
123. Answers may vary.
124. Answers may vary.
125. My sister's friend lost a tooth.

Bonus Builder #25:
    dr. Benjamin D. Levine   Mr. john Bragg
    (Miss Emily Taggart)   (Dr. Timersol)
    mrs. sheehan

Answer Keys

Page 28

126. Answers may vary.
127. seven
128. Answers may vary.
129. The pretty brown horse trotted through the meadow.
130. Ouch, my toe hurts?
     Did you remember to feed the dog?
     Can you fly a kite?

Bonus Builder #26: Answers may vary.

Page 29

131. Answers may vary for additional words. Examples:
     trap—train, trick   smile—smart, smell
     stop—start, stem   flip—flag, flower
     from—frog, frame
132. a whale; Drawings may vary.
133. Answers may vary. (Examples: on a desk, at school, in an airport,
     in a bank, in a car)
134. Answers may vary. (Examples: kind, funny, big, skinny, tall)
135. On Friday it was snowing so hard that I couldn't see out the
     window.

Bonus Builder #27:
     I ate and ate off my p l a t e .
     I fell on the floor, then ran out the d o o r !
     I cracked an egg on my l e g .
     You're so bright, that I know you're r i g h t !

Page 30

136. Answers may vary. (Examples: coat, wrote, float, tote, goat)
137. **X** Nick and Kari ran in the waves.
     X They made a sand castle.
        The horse ran into the barn.
     X We ate a picnic lunch on the sand.
138. Answers may vary.
139. Wow, that fish is huge!
     I like to fish in the pond.
140. dr., america, flag, washington, chicago

Bonus Builder #28: Answers may vary.

Page 31

141. going, playing, making, running, coming, jumping
142. pigs
143. Answers may vary.
144. little, small, pretty, tiny, funny, huge
145. Wow, look at that pretty flower!
     Did you lose a tooth yesterday?

Bonus Builder #29:
     1. barn
     2. corn

Page 32

146. ★ like   sed—said or seed
     hav—have   ★ you
     ★ look   du—do
147.
A	B
The little bird	walked to the store.
The man	swam in the water.
The pretty fish	flew to its nest.

148. Answers may vary.
149. boys, foxes, eyes, wishes, churches
150. jane smith
     414 main street
     jonesburg, virginia 41433

Bonus Builder #30:
     r e (p l a t e) d
     l m (k i t e) m n
     r f i d (f e e t)
     m n (h o p e) w s
     (m u l e) p o d c

Page 33

151. well, under, say, be, stop, just
152. Drawings should match description.
153. Answers may vary.
154. Answers may vary.
155. Yesterday I ate a ham, burger, french, fries, and a milk, shake.
     ★ Yesterday I ate a hamburger, french fries, and a milkshake.

Bonus Builder #31:
     Chocolate is the best flavor for ice cream.
     Robins can fly.
     Mr. Smith is the kindest teacher in the school.
     January is the nicest month of the year.

Page 34

156. Answers may vary for word choices. Examples:
     sw ing—sweep, sway
     bl ue—black, blade
     pr ince—pride, prune
     gr ay—green, grass
     sk in—skip, sky
157. The Busy Horse
     The Red Barn
     A Pretty Meadow
158. Answers may vary.
159. dishes, gas, girls, car, tires
160. Tom asked, "Would you like to go to the zoo with me?"

Bonus Builder #32
     I would like to have (a, an) dog.
     Will you eat (a, an) banana?
     I have (a, an) earache.
     I saw (a, an) elephant at the zoo.

Page 35

161. Answers may vary. Examples:
     mile—male, mole, mule
     tame—time
     cone—cane
     mine—mane
     lake—like
162. They have four, six, or eight eyes.
     No, spiders are arachnids.
163. Answers may vary.
164. ★ My brother broke his leg.
     My sister is swimming in the lake.
165. Joe, Tim, Ron, and Nan went to the store to buy balloons, plates,
     cups, and spoons.

Bonus Builder #33: Answers may vary.

Page 36

166. Nan didn't eat her apple. did not
     Fran can't see the bus. can not
     It's Dan's birthday today. it is
167. not telling the truth
168. Answers may vary.
169. Sue's dresses are all red.
     That's my ball.
170. Wonce I saw a liddle bird fli away frum a cat.

Bonus Builder #34: furry, happy, black, quickly, loud

Answer Keys

Page 37

171. rid(e)   pla(y)
     bo(a)t   pa(i)d
     mak(e)
172. water
173. Answers may vary.
174. Will you <u>play</u> with me?
     <u>I want to go see the play</u>.
175. Would you like to take a trip to Hawaii, California, or Florida?

Bonus Builder #35:
     The <u>night</u> helped the queen.   (I don't <u>know</u> the answer.)
     (The moon can be seen at <u>night</u>.)   I have <u>know</u> more paper.

Page 38

176. I came (here) to (hear) the band play.
177. Answers may vary. Examples:
     Once there was a little frog. The <u>frog</u> did not like to jump. The frog did not <u>like</u> to hop. Day after <u>day</u> the little frog just sat on a lily pad. The <u>little</u> frog did nothing but catch flies!
178. Answers may vary.
179. (Jill ate four red apples.)
     Josh walked three blocks.
180. How old will you be on your next birthday?
     What time is it?
     My father likes to bake bread.

Bonus Builder #36:
     (There are twelve months in a year.)
     Pizza House makes the best pizza!
     Snickers® is the best candy bar.
     (George Washington was the first president.)

Page 39

181. big — huge
     funny — silly
     small — tiny
     scared — frightened
     sick — ill
182. Pour in the water and stir.
183. Answers may vary.
184. Answers may vary. (Examples: slowly, safely, calmly)
185. I ordered a sundae with syrup, whipped cream, nuts, sprinkles, and a cherry on top.

Bonus Builder #37:
     My brother is <u>two</u> years old.
     I am going <u>to</u> a party.
     She will go to the party, <u>too</u>!

Page 40

186. it's—it is   we'll—we will
     can't—can not   won't—will not
     she'll—she will
187. a princess
188. Answers may vary.
189. (Chip plays in the woods.)
     Kari fell out of bed last night.
     (He reads books.)
190. There should be quotation marks before the word *please* and after the period. The *p* in please should be capitalized.

Bonus Builder #38: Answers may vary.

Page 41

191. summer—2
     rain—1
     apple—2
     wagon—2
     envelope—3
192. at a bus station
193. Answers may vary.
194. Victor put _____ cake in the oven.
     (his)   I
     Mrs. Conor took _____ sister to a party.
     she   (her)
195. My grandmother made cookies, cake, and lemonade.

Bonus Builder #39:
     (cent)
     (celery)
     carrot
     cable
     (pace)

Page 42

196. (weed)   (tree)
     (seat)   toe
     pail   tube
197. at the beach
198. Answers may vary.
199. Tomas ~~he~~ cleaned his fish tank.
     Alex doesn't ~~not~~ have his own room.
200. anser
     (answer)
     ansor

Bonus Builder #40:
     bote   (boat)
     (snail)   snale
     (tube)   toob
     trea   (tree)

Page 43

201. is not—isn't
     they are—they're
     it is—it's
     he will—he'll
     have not—haven't
     will not—won't
202. fantasy
203. Answers may vary.
204. bus, (mice), (boxes), clock, (cars)
205. Jamal (talking) on the phone for an hour.
     Tony put on his helmet and (ride) his bike.
     Amy is (swims) faster than Carl. (The word *is* could be circled instead.)

Bonus Builder #41: horse; It is not a describing word (adjective).

Page 44

206. (broad), moat, (hoad), <u>otoam</u>, <u>droam</u>
207. memorized
208. Answers may vary.
209. Jordan [quickly] stood up.
     Max walked [slowly] to the front of the room.
     Andrew [smoothly] spread the frosting on the cake.
210. (The brown dog ran quickly to the park.)
     my best friend jan ran quickly around the playground

Bonus Builder #42: soup, (couch), (cloud), cold